THE
MEANING
OF
MARRIAGE
Study Guide

Other Studies by Timothy Keller

Gospel in Life (video and study guide)

Jesus the King (study guide only)

The Prodigal God (video and study guide)

The Reason for God (video and study guide)

New York Times **Bestselling Author of**
THE REASON FOR GOD **and** *THE PRODIGAL GOD*

THE
MEANING
OF
MARRIAGE
Study Guide

A Vision for Married and Single People

TIMOTHY and KATHY KELLER
and SPENCE SHELTON

ZONDERVAN

The Meaning of Marriage Study Guide
Copyright © 2015 by Redeemer City to City

This title is also available as a Zondervan ebook. Visit www.zondervan.com/ebooks.

Requests for information should be addressed to:

Zondervan, 3900 *Sparks Dr. SE, Grand Rapids, Michigan 49546*

ISBN 978-0-310-86825-5

Producer/editors: Scott Kauffmann, Mai Hariu-Powell
Cover design: Richard Hasselberger
Interior design: Matthew Van Zomeren

First Printing July 2015 / Printed in the United States of America
16 17 18 19 20 /DCI/ 20 19 18 17 16 15 14 13 12 11 10 9 8

CONTENTS

Ephesians 5:22–33

Wives, submit yourselves to your own husbands as you do to the Lord. 23 For the husband is the head of the wife as Christ is the head of the church, his body, of which he is the Savior. 24 Now as the church submits to Christ, so also wives should submit to their husbands in everything.

25 Husbands, love your wives, just as Christ loved the church and gave himself up for her 26 to make her holy, cleansing her by the washing with water through the word, 27 and to present her to himself as a radiant church, without stain or wrinkle or any other blemish, but holy and blameless. 28 In this same way, husbands ought to love their wives as their own bodies. He who loves his wife loves himself. 29 After all, no one ever hated their own body, but they feed and care for their body, just as Christ does the church — 30 for we are members of his body. 31 "For this reason a man will leave his father and mother and be united to his wife, and the two will become one flesh." 32 This is a profound mystery — but I am talking about Christ and the church. 33 However, each one of you also must love his wife as he loves himself, and the wife must respect her husband.

INTRODUCTION

Love is as strong as death,
its jealousy unyielding as the grave.
It burns like blazing fire,
like a mighty flame.
Many waters cannot quench love;
rivers cannot sweep it away.
If one were to give
all the wealth of one's house for love,
it would be utterly scorned.

—King Solomon (Song of Songs 8:6–7)

We are obsessed with love. Our Billboard charts, movie theaters, and all of our screens pile stories upon stories about our longing to love and be loved. The greatest novels and plays of all cultures in all times are filled with love stories. Some are tragic and some end in happily ever after, but every culture has love stories because love is at the core of the human experience. Simply put, we are always pursuing and longing for love.

Over time and through a variety of big and small moments in marriage, you will encounter many of your life's greatest joys and sternest tests. That is why most married people will tell you that marriage is hard work—because in marriage you are regularly handling the powerful forces of selfishness and love, and that requires patience, hope, repentance, forgiveness, and great intentionality.

The primary goal of this study is to help all of us, regardless of our marital status, to see the marriage covenant as a reflection of Jesus' love, grace, and power in our lives. In these sessions you will explore the profound mystery of the love described by the apostle Paul in his letter to the Ephesian church. There he shows us that the love of God, given to us in the gospel, is the only inexhaustible source for sacrificial love between spouses—as it is for all human love in general.

After all, the climactic "I do" in a wedding ceremony seals more than just a romantic moment. It is a public promise to love our spouse in a way that can only happen through knowing Jesus as our ultimate, true spouse. But that will involve a reconstruction of the way most of us have been taught to think about marriage, singleness, and love.

We hope discussion groups will go through this material together because truth is transformative when processed in community—and we encourage you to include both married and single people in that community as you work through the material.

HOW TO USE
THIS STUDY

The Meaning of Marriage is a six-session video study designed for small groups but adaptable for use by couples and individuals, both married and single. The video sessions are facilitated by Jeff White, a pastor at Redeemer Presbyterian Church in Manhattan, and feature Tim and Kathy Keller and participants with a variety of spiritual beliefs and life experiences in both marriage and singleness. All participants read the book and reread certain chapters in preparation for the filmed discussions. We are grateful for each of their voices and thoughtful perspectives in these discussions, and we hope their insights will fuel similar dialogue in your group as well.

WHAT YOU WILL NEED

In addition to *The Meaning of Marriage* DVD (one per group) and this study guide, each person or couple will need the following:

A copy of the book *The Meaning of Marriage.* While the Group Times are designed so that you can participate without this book, you will need this book for your Home Study. (Page numbers noted throughout this study guide are from the paperback edition, Riverhead Books, 2013.)

A Bible. If you don't have a copy, there are plenty of free apps you can use to download a free copy of the Bible. You will have the opportunity to read sections of the Bible throughout these next six weeks as a central part of this experience.

EACH SESSION HAS THREE COMPONENTS

1. Home Study

To get the most out of this experience you will interact with concepts before, during, and after your group gathering. Each Home Study is designed to help you reflect on the content from your most recent Group Time, and then prepare for the upcoming session by reading and reflecting on a selected chapter or two from *The Meaning of Marriage*.

2. Group Time

The Group Time component walks a small group through key concepts from the book *The Meaning of Marriage*. Each group discussion will include a video (about 20–25 minutes long) that covers selected ideas from each chapter. The study guide will then lead your group through a discussion to help you apply the principles from the book, the video, and your Home Study. Most questions are relevant to both married and single people; a few in each session apply only to married people.

3. Marriage Plan

In addition to the Home Study and Group Time, an exercise specifically for married couples is built into each session. These exercises —designed to do at home or on a date—will help married couples apply what they are learning in practical ways.

NOTES FOR LEADERS

If you are leading the discussions, please see the Notes for Leaders section in the back of this guide for helpful commentary on various questions.

GETTING READY FOR SESSION 1

Please read chapters 1–2 of *The Meaning of Marriage* before your first Group Time. This will set your group on a good pace to cover the entire book by the end of the study.

SERVICE
Marriage Isn't about You

HOME STUDY

The Introduction is best read individually, as a part of your Home Study, in preparation for your Group Time. Also read chapters 1–2, "The Secret of Marriage" and "The Power for Marriage," in The Meaning of Marriage *if you haven't already.*

INTRODUCTION

"I do." The most romantic, hope-filled climax of any wedding ceremony is when the bride and groom utter that two-word phrase, "I do," that launches their life together. The whole ceremony builds to those vows of commitment, and the festivities to follow celebrate them. Such a rich, intimate relationship as marriage deserves the pomp and circumstance it often receives on the wedding day. Yet for all the attention the wedding gets, most married couples agree that in addition to their coordinated wedding attire they were also unknowingly wearing blinders. These invisible blinders shielded them from a full understanding of what was to come in the marriage relationship.

Most people come into marriage with a set of expectations. Sometimes verbalized but most often not, these expectations create a grid you and your spouse will use to evaluate the happiness and overall quality of your marriage. Your culture and experiences help to create, and to reinforce, these expectations. When these hopes are met, the facade of a happy life holds up. But inevitably the day will come when married life will not live up to your expectations. Maybe it will be over something small—like who should pay the bills and manage the household finances; or maybe it will be something weightier—like a job loss, a pornography addiction, unexpected medical expenses, or a child on the wrong track. In some form, reality will eventually disappoint your expectations for marriage. Because the future is unknown and the possibilities are endless, no quick fix (a date night, a budget, etc.) will ever be thorough or specific enough to help you through every circumstance. Marriages will need a constant reorientation to the meaning of marriage.

What if your marriage had a foundation that allowed it to flourish even, and maybe especially in, the disappointing spaces of life? The goal of this session is to sharpen your vision for such a life-giving foundation for your marriage.

GROUP TIME

WELCOME/OPENING QUESTIONS

To begin this first session, take a moment to get to know one another. As you introduce yourselves, share what you hope to gain from this study. Then spend a few minutes exploring the following questions. There are no right or wrong answers, so relax! And not everyone need feel obligated to answer.

What were some expectations you had (or have, if you are single) about what marriage should be like?

How have those expectations helped or hurt your understanding of marriage?

VIDEO PRESENTATION

*Watch the video for Session 1: "Service: Marriage Isn't about You."
Use the space provided to take notes on any ideas that stand out to you.
Your discussion to follow will review and seek to apply the main ideas
of the session.*

Notes

DISCUSSION

The following questions are designed to help the group process the ideas from the video, the Bible, and chapters 1 and 2 of the book The Meaning of Marriage. *The goal is to begin applying these ideas to your life.*

1. What from the video discussion resonated with you as key principles for marriage?

2. In the discussion Jeff asked the group, "Why is service so important to marriage?" Though counterintuitive, the Christian worldview says the key to building a happy and fulfilling marriage is through mutual sacrifice. How does the idea that it is "not about you" actually help you build a healthy marriage? How has selfishness worked against this idea in your marriage?

3. In the discussion, Tim said that marriage has both horizontal and vertical dimensions. The purpose of the horizontal dimension—our relationships with other people—is character change and community building. The vertical dimension—our relationship with Jesus—fuels us to serve our horizontal relationships. In what ways has your vertical relationship with Jesus affected your horizontal relationship with others?

4. What has helped you keep your relationship with God as the primary love relationship in your life? In what ways can your friends, spouse, and those in your community help you, and how can you help them?

5. Kristin said that if she only had the horizontal dimension and not the vertical in her marriage, she couldn't "hold up under the burden of what Joe needs." What are ways to make sure we are not expecting other people to meet the needs that only God can fulfill?

6. Toward the end of the discussion, Sam said he found the Christian approach to marriage to be "enviable." How does the gospel offer an attractive foundation for marriage?

> This is the secret—that the gospel of Jesus and marriage explain one another. That when God invented marriage, he already had the saving work of Jesus in mind.
>
> *The Meaning of Marriage*, p. 43

7. In the concluding remarks, Kathy summed up the Christian approach to marriage as "gospel reenactment." That is, the interactions between the husband and wife are to serve as a dynamic retelling of the story of Christ's love and sacrifice for the church.

In your own words, explain what the gospel is. (Use Ephesians 2:1–10, printed below, to guide you if necessary.)

As for you, you were dead in your transgressions and sins, [2] in which you used to live when you followed the ways of this world and of the ruler of the kingdom of the air, the spirit who is now at work in those who are disobedient. [3] All of us also lived among them at one time, gratifying the cravings of our flesh and following its desires and thoughts. Like the rest, we were by nature deserving of wrath.[4] But because of his great love for us, God, who is rich in mercy, [5] made us alive with Christ even when we were dead in transgressions—it is by grace you have been saved. [6] And God raised us up with Christ and seated us with him in the heavenly realms in Christ Jesus, [7] in order that in the coming ages he might show the incomparable riches of his grace, expressed in his kindness to us in Christ Jesus. [8] For it is by grace you have been saved, through faith—and this is not from yourselves, it is the gift of God—[9] not by works, so that no one can boast. [10] For we are God's handiwork, created in Christ Jesus to do good works, which God prepared in advance for us to do.

Ephesians 2:1–10

How would you explain the phrase "gospel reenactment"?

> The Christian teaching does not offer a choice between fulfillment and sacrifice but mutual fulfillment through mutual sacrifice.
>
> *The Meaning of Marriage*, p. 43

8. Give an example of what gospel reenactment could look like in the regular weekly rhythms of your marriage. If you are not married, what could gospel reenactment look like in the key relationships in your life?

CLOSING PRAYER

Close your discussion by praying together as a group, asking with grace and humility for God's help in applying what you've learned in this session.

HOME STUDY

PERSONAL REFLECTION

There, then, is the message of this book—that through marriage, "the mystery of the gospel is unveiled." Marriage is a major vehicle for the gospel's remaking of your heart from the inside out and your life from the ground up.

The reason that marriage is so painful and yet wonderful is because it is a reflection of the gospel, which is painful and wonderful at once. The gospel is this: We are more sinful and flawed in ourselves than we ever dared believe, yet at the very same time we are more loved and accepted in Jesus Christ than we ever dared hope....

The gospel can fill our hearts with God's love so that you can handle it when your spouse fails to love you as he or she should. That frees us to see our spouse's sins and flaws to the bottom—and speak of them—and yet still love and accept our spouse fully. And when, by the power of the gospel, our spouse experiences that same kind of truthful yet committed love, it enables our spouses to show us that same kind of transforming love when the time comes for it.

This is the great secret! Through the gospel, we get both the power and the pattern for the journey of marriage.

The Meaning of Marriage, pp. 44–45

1. Where do you stand in relation to the Christian faith commitment? At this point do you fully believe the gospel message, as described in this session? Are there any questions you have about the gospel or its implications?

2. In the video, Tim said Christianity is an identity and that "if I believe in the Christian gospel, I realize I am living by the commitment of someone who sacrificed for me. So how dare I live on that and accept that and not give it to anybody else?" In light of this session, do you sense anything you need to adjust about the way you are approaching your spouse and others in your life?

READ FOR NEXT TIME

Read chapter 3, "The Essence of Marriage," and chapter 5, "Loving the Stranger," in *The Meaning of Marriage* along with the letter to the Ephesians found in the New Testament. Also read the Introduction to the next session, "Covenant: Created to Make Promises."

MARRIAGE PLAN

This entire study is designed to be a tool to help strengthen marriages. When you complete *The Meaning of Marriage* curriculum, you will have the beginnings of a marriage plan you can begin to pursue as a couple. These conversations are best to have while out on a date so you can avoid many of your normal distractions. Here is your exercise for this week:

HOW CAN I SERVE YOU?

Our (Spence's) church recently went through a focused season on marriage, during which we were confronted with the selfless love of Christ as the model for how spouses are to love one another. Christ not only submitted himself to God the Father when he came to earth, but he also seemed to place himself in a posture of always serving the disciples. The most poignant example—when Jesus washed the disciples' feet—is a major reinforcement of the simple truth he proclaimed that "the Son of Man did not come to be served, but to serve, and to give his life as a ransom for many" (Mark 10:45). So, as a church, we crafted the simplest of exercises that has greatly benefited my marriage and many others. Here it is:

Step 1: Ask your spouse, "What can I do to serve you?"
Step 2: If within reason, do what your spouse requests.
Step 3: Repeat often.

This simple question "What can I do to serve you?" will feel a little forced and silly at first. But if you play along, eventually it can be one of those small steps God uses to unlock the power of the gospel in your marriage. So, while out on the date, discuss the following three questions:

1. What can I do to serve you this week?

2. What can I do to help you love God and be refueled in his love this week?

3. Are there any big-picture areas in our lives where I can serve you and our family?

COVENANT
Created to Make Promises

HOME STUDY

Read the Introduction in preparation for the Session 2 Group Time. Also read chapter 3, "The Essence of Marriage," and chapter 5, "Loving the Stranger," in The Meaning of Marriage *and the New Testament book of Ephesians if you haven't already.*

INTRODUCTION

When the dust settled at the end of the Revolutionary War, the American colonies found themselves trying to figure out how to build the free country they had fought so hard to attain. Though Francis Scott Key wouldn't coin the phrase "land of the free" until 1812, the ethos of freedom was absolutely central to the new America of 1776.

In order for America to be a free and prosperous nation, her citizens had to commit themselves to a new form of governance. Unless they gave one another the mutual trust needed to submit to a new governing system, the fledgling country would be unstable, fair game for any faction to rise up and overtake it. It was, ironically enough, their voluntary commitment to binding laws that set these new "Americans" free and made their union strong.

Many people in our day look at the marriage commitment as restrictive to their individual freedoms. Once married, your new spouse becomes "the old ball and chain" who will shackle you from experiencing the full enjoyment the single life once offered you. Yet the biblical perspective on marriage portrays this commitment as essential to finding deep freedom. In fact, it is the binding promise, or covenant, that creates the freedom people search for. By looking closely at the marriage covenant, this session intends to upend the common contemporary view of marriage as confining and archaic, and to unveil the great hope and freedom marriage offers.

GROUP TIME

REVIEW

The first session, "Service: Marriage Isn't about You," emphasized the selfless nature of the gospel and how it serves as a model and motivation for serving your spouse throughout your years of marriage. Putting the principle of sacrificial love into practice in marriage is what the Kellers called "gospel reenactment."

This gospel reenactment is about serving one another in the same way Christ served the church in his death and resurrection for her.

- Did you have any follow-up conversations or reactions to the ideas presented in Session 1?
- What significant takeaways did you have from your reading and reflection during your Home Study?

OPENING QUESTION

Written or not, everyone has some version of a list when looking for "Mr. or Mrs. Right." If you're married, what things were on your list beforehand? If you're not married, what things would be on your list now?

VIDEO PRESENTATION

Watch the video for Session 2: "Covenant: Created to Make Promises." Use the space provided to take notes on any ideas that stand out to you. Your discussion to follow will review and seek to apply the main ideas of the session.

Notes

DISCUSSION

The following questions are designed to help the group process the ideas from the video, the Bible, and chapters 3 and 5 of the book The Meaning of Marriage. *The goal is to begin applying these ideas to your life.*

1. Did you hear anything in the video that was particularly helpful? Was there anything that you disagreed with?

2. Tim explained three things that should be on everyone's list of desired traits in a spouse:

   a. *A common worldview:* What do we think human beings are for? How do we decide right and wrong? When we die, what happens?
   b. *Ability to solve problems:* How do we solve problems? Do we "fight well"?
   c. *Shared mythos:* Do we share a "secret thread" of things that move us deeply and fill us with joy?

   What is your reaction to this list? How does one discover these traits in another person?

3. Sam asked, "What makes the Christian vows unique?" This is a very reasonable and practical question that anyone — Christian or otherwise — should ask. What was helpful in the video responses? How would you answer Sam's question?

4. God describes his relationship with his people through the term "covenant," as seen in passages such as Genesis 17:3 – 7 and Ezekiel 37:26 – 28 (printed below). Using these two passages, describe what God means by the word "covenant" when using it to talk about his relationship to his people.

> Abram fell facedown, and God said to him, ⁴ "As for me, this is my covenant with you: You will be the father of many nations. ⁵ No longer will you be called Abram; your name will be Abraham, for I have made you a father of many nations. ⁶ I will make you very fruitful; I will make nations of you, and kings will come from you. ⁷ I will establish my covenant as an everlasting covenant between me and you and your descendants after you for the generations to come, to be your God and the God of your descendants after you."   Genesis 17:3 – 7

> I will make a covenant of peace with them; it will be an everlasting covenant. I will establish them and increase their numbers, and I will put my sanctuary among them forever. ²⁷ My dwelling place will be with them; I will be their God, and they will be my people. ²⁸ Then the nations will know that I the LORD make Israel holy, when my sanctuary is among them forever.   Ezekiel 37:26 – 28

5. Genesis 2:22–25 and Malachi 2:14 (printed below) are two Scripture passages that depict marriage as a covenant. The Genesis passage describes it and the Malachi passage labels it. Based on what "covenant" means in the Bible, what does it mean for God to use the word to define marriage?

> Then the LORD God made a woman from the rib he had taken out of the man, and he brought her to the man. 23 The man said, "This is now bone of my bones and flesh of my flesh; she shall be called 'woman,' for she was taken out of man." 24 That is why a man leaves his father and mother and is united to his wife, and they become one flesh. 25 Adam and his wife were both naked, and they felt no shame.
>
> Genesis 2:22–25

> You ask, "Why?" It is because the LORD is the witness between you and the wife of your youth. You have been unfaithful to her, though she is your partner, *the wife of your marriage covenant.*
>
> Malachi 2:14, emphasis added

> [In the marriage promise] "you have created a small sanctuary of trust within the jungle of unpredictability."
> Lewis Smedes, quoted in *The Meaning of Marriage*, p. 98

6. How does the "sanctuary of trust" of the marriage covenant offer greater freedom than one can find outside of it?

> Marriage has the power of truth, the ability to reveal to you who you really are, with all your flaws. How wonderful that it also has the "power of love"—an unmatched power to affirm you and heal you of the deepest wounds and hurts of your life.
>
> *The Meaning of Marriage*, p. 162

7. The power of truth and love inside a marriage can be incredibly strong, either positively formative or negatively destructive. Why is the affirming love of a spouse so powerful?

8. How can the dynamic of affirming love and fulfillment work on a practical level for a single person?

CLOSING PRAYER

Close your discussion by praying together as a group, asking with grace and humility for God's help in applying what you've learned in this session.

HOME STUDY

The Home Study provides you an opportunity to reconnect with the ideas from the most recent session and to prepare for the next one. Your experience in Group Time will be greatly enhanced when each person completes the Home Study between sessions.

PERSONAL REFLECTION

Read the following excerpt from The Meaning of Marriage *and then answer the questions provided.*

And there's the Great Problem of marriage. The one person in the whole world who holds your heart in her hand, whose approval and affirmation you most long for and need, is the one who is hurt more deeply by your sins than anyone else on the planet. When we are first sinned against by our spouses in a serious way, we use the power of truth. We tell our spouses what fools, what messes, what selfish pigs they are....

When we see how devastating truth-telling in marriage can be, it can push us into the opposite error. We may then decide that our job is to just affirm.... We stuff and hide what we really think and feel. We exercise the power of love, but not the power of truth....

Truth without love ruins oneness, and love without truth gives the illusion of unity but actually stops the journey and the growth. The solution is grace. The experience of Jesus's grace makes it possible to practice the two most important skills in marriage: forgiveness and repentance. Only if we are very good at forgiving and very good at repenting can truth and love be kept together....

One of the most basic skills in marriage is the ability to tell the straight, unvarnished truth about what your spouse has done—and then, completely, unself-righteously, and joyously express forgiveness without a shred of superiority, without making the other person feel small. This does not mean you cannot express anger. In fact, if you never express anger, your truth-telling probably won't sink in. But forgiving grace must always be present, and if it is, it will, like salt in meat, keep the anger from going bad. Then truth and love can live together because, beneath them both, you have forgiven your spouse as Christ forgave you.

The Meaning of Marriage, pp. 180–81, 182, 183–84

1. In general, how would you characterize the way you forgive others, seek forgiveness, and repent with others? With your spouse?

2. What action step may God be leading you to take with your spouse, or another loved one, in response to this session?

READ FOR NEXT TIME

Read chapter 6, "Embracing the Other," in *The Meaning of Marriage*. Also read the Introduction to the next session, "Roles: Loving through Mutual Submission."

MARRIAGE PLAN

To be completed as a couple between group sessions, preferably while out on a date away from the normal distractions of life.

GETTING ON THE SAME CHANNEL

In chapter 5 of *The Meaning of Marriage*, Tim uses the metaphor of radio frequencies to describe a type of communication trouble many married couples encounter. Though a message might be sent out on one radio frequency, if the receiver is not set to the same frequency, the message will never be received. A necessary learning curve in marriage involves getting on the same frequency with how you give and receive love. A great way to display the love you have for your spouse is to humble yourself enough to study how he or she best receives your acts of love.

The human heart is a complex thing that we do not want to reduce to a formula. This exercise is simply designed to help you discuss how God has wired you so that you can begin operating on the same frequency in your marriage. Once out on your date, discuss the following questions:

1. If your boss were going to reward you for a job well done, how would you prefer he or she do it? Why?

    a. With a handwritten personal note and a gift card to your favorite restaurant
    b. With a bonus check
    c. Acknowledgment at the next large company staff meeting
    d. Two words: vacation days

2. In the book, the Kellers talked about three ways people prefer to be loved.* Some respond best to physical and verbal affection, others to close friendship, and still others to acts of service. Based on what you know about yourself and your spouse, answer the following questions separately, then discuss your answers.

Complete this sentence: The way I will best receive a loving gesture is if it...

Why did you write that?

Complete this sentence: The way my spouse will best receive a loving gesture is if it...

Why did you write that?

---

* For more on understanding your spouse's "love language," consider reading Gary Chapman's classic book *The Five Love Languages* (Northfield).

ROLES
Loving through Mutual Submission

HOME STUDY

Read the Introduction in preparation for the Session 3 Group Time. Also read chapter 6, "Embracing the Other," in The Meaning of Marriage *if you haven't already.*

INTRODUCTION

No topic is likely to elicit a wider range of reactions and emotions in this entire group experience than gender roles. There are several factors that make this discussion both extremely important and potentially uneasy for Christians to navigate. If you are to walk through them successfully in this session, you must first acknowledge what makes this aspect of marriage so difficult for people in the West today.

Principles over prescriptions. As you will see in this session, the Bible focuses on the principles of gender roles and seems less concerned about the specific practices each spouse is supposed to carry out. For many who want a straightforward "just tell me the rule" answer, the hard work of faithfully interpreting a biblical principle and applying it to our context is confusing and sometimes frustrating. That said, the Bible says what it says for a reason. When we rightly understand what the Bible says, we will start to unlock the kind of freedom we deeply crave.

It's personal. Spouses bring their histories into every aspect of marriage. One aspect where our history is most influential is what we believe to be the other person's role in the marriage. Personal history makes emotions run high, and every married person has a critical stake in this conversation. Whatever you choose to believe about marriage roles and mutual submission will directly influence what you do and how you do it on a daily basis in your married life.

It's countercultural. To even broach the subject of gender distinctions reveals a rift between the Christian worldview and the predominant worldview in the West today. Whether because of outdated reputations about "the church" or because of bad firsthand or secondhand experiences, or of differing views on the question of gender identity altogether, many raise a red flag as soon as they hear the subject. If that describes you, we are glad you are here and hope you feel this is a safe place to engage the conversation. We can only ask you to hear out the discussion and weigh what the Bible has to say, together with people you trust.

For these reasons and many more, many Christians have relegated gender roles to the "break glass in case of emergency" box. Which means they only employ their God-given marriage roles if and when the two spouses disagree on a major decision, like a potential career change or home move. In case of such an emergency, you break the glass to retrieve the Marriage Decision Tiebreaking instructions. Others fear that the notion of roles in marriage is a social construct creating a "box" they will be pressured into. They don't want to be told they have to assimilate into a set of wifely or husbandly duties just because their time and place in a culture expects them to.

What if the husband-and-wife roles were actually empowering for everyday life rather than confining? Just as service can be a joy rather than a burden, and promises can set you free rather than bind you, leaning into your distinct role in your marriage can be liberating rather than limiting. We believe that fully embracing the role God gave you as a man or woman in marriage will not only cause your marriage to flourish but will help turn you into the person God created you to be.

GROUP TIME

REVIEW

Session 2, "Covenant: Created to Make Promises," focused on the covenantal nature of marriage. The big idea was that God's covenant with humankind becomes the source and model for the commitment between a husband and wife.

- How has your experience been so far with your Marriage Plan exercises?
- What ideas or lessons did you discover or see again through your Home Study about the power of repentance and forgiveness?

OPENING QUESTION

Following is a "no wrong answer" question designed to get everyone talking. This particular session's content is hotly debated in our present day, and it is likely group members will bring different stories to the table.

This session will dive into gender roles in marriage and the concept of mutual submission between spouses. Think back to your childhood. What roles did your mom play? What roles did your dad play? If one or both were not in the picture, who played what roles in your home life?

VIDEO PRESENTATION

Watch the video for Session 3: "Roles: Loving through Mutual Submission." Use the space provided to take notes on any ideas that stand out to you. Your discussion to follow will review and seek to apply the main ideas of the session.

Notes

DISCUSSION

The following questions are designed to help the group process the ideas from the video, the Bible, and chapter 6 of the book The Meaning of Marriage. *The goal is to begin applying these ideas to your life.*

1. What comment or thought from the video did you think was helpful in clarifying the biblical understanding of gender roles in marriage? Were there surprises?

2. This session asserted that the Bible is clear that men and women are of equal value and glory and have different roles (leader and helper), yet the Bible doesn't say what specific tasks, skills, or temperaments belong to each of those roles. How does this challenge the way you've observed and/or approached marriage to this point?

3. Every individual has a different experience in their role as a husband or wife. Are there any areas in your marriage where you feel your role comes naturally to you? Are there any ways you feel you operate counter to the typical expectations of your role?

> Both women *and* men get to "play the Jesus role" in marriage—Jesus in his sacrificial authority, Jesus in his sacrificial submission. By accepting our gender roles, and operating within them, we are able to demonstrate to the world concepts that are so counterintuitive as to be completely unintelligible unless they are lived out by men and women in Christian marriages.
>
> *The Meaning of Marriage*, pp. 201–2

4. In the video and in the reading, the idea was proposed that both spouses get to play "Jesus roles." That is, each spouse reflects the person and work of Jesus in unique ways through the roles they are designed to play. If both roles are primarily designed to reflect Christ, then both must hold equal value in the marriage. This idea came from a comparison of our anchor passage in this study, Ephesians 5:22–33, with Philippians 2:5–11.

Read Ephesians 5:25–33 (printed below). How is the husband's role as the leader in the marriage a "Jesus role"?

Husbands, love your wives, just as Christ loved the church and gave himself up for her [26] to make her holy, cleansing her by the washing with water through the word, [27] and to present her to himself as a radiant church, without stain or wrinkle or any other blemish, but holy and blameless. [28] In this same way, husbands ought to love their wives as their own bodies. He who loves his wife loves himself. [29] After all, no one ever hated their own body, but they feed and care for their body, just as Christ does the church — [30] for we are members of his body. [31] "For this reason a man will leave his father and mother and be united to his wife, and the two will become one flesh." [32] This is a profound mystery — but I am talking about Christ and the church. [33] However, each one of you also must love his wife as he loves himself, and the wife must respect her husband.   Ephesians 5:25 – 33

Read Philippians 2:5 – 11 (printed below). How is the wife's role in submission to her husband a "Jesus role"?

In your relationships with one another, have the same mindset as Christ Jesus: [6] Who, being in very nature God, did not consider equality with God something to be used to his own advantage; [7] rather, he made himself nothing by taking the very nature of a servant, being made in human likeness. [8] And being found in appearance as a man, he humbled himself by becoming obedient to death — even death on a cross!

[9] Therefore God exalted him to the highest place and gave him the name that is above every name, [10] that at the name of Jesus every knee should bow, in heaven and on earth and under the earth, [11] and every tongue acknowledge that Jesus Christ is Lord, to the glory of God the Father.   Philippians 2:5–11

> The external details of a family's division of labor may be worked out differently across marriages and societies. But the tender, serving authority of a husband's headship and the strong, gracious gift of a wife's submission restore us to who we were meant to be at creation.
>
> *The Meaning of Marriage*, p. 208

5. In your own words, explain the concept of "mutual submission" and why it's so important to a healthy "gospel reenactment" in marriage. What are some ways to seek accountability and learn communally on doing mutual submission and gospel reenactment well?

6. How might God be calling you to embrace your gender role as a way of becoming the person God wants you to be, even if it is uncomfortable for you?

7. As Steve mentioned in the video, gender roles certainly seem irrelevant to the single person. But in what ways is it helpful in everyday life for a single person to understand gender roles? Along the lines of Tina's example, in what ways can single men and women honor one another in community?

CLOSING PRAYER

Close your discussion by praying together as a group, asking with grace and humility for God's help in applying what you've learned in this session.

HOME STUDY

The Home Study provides you an opportunity to reconnect with the ideas from the most recent session and to prepare for the next one. Your experience in Group Time will be greatly enhanced when each person completes the Home Study between sessions.

PERSONAL REFLECTION

Read the following excerpt below from The Meaning of Marriage *and then answer the questions provided.*

Miroslav Volf, writing in *Exclusion and Embrace*, shows that the God of the Bible embraces the Other, and it is us. Quoting another theologian, Volf writes:

> "On the cross of Christ [the love of God] is there for the others, for sinners—the recalcitrant—enemies. The reciprocal self-surrender to one another within the Trinity is manifested in Christ's self-surrender in a world which is in contradiction to God; and this self-giving draws all those who believe in him into the eternal life of divine love."

Christ embraced the ultimate "Other"—sinful humanity. He didn't exclude us by simply consigning us to judgment. He embraced us by dying on the cross for our sins. To love the Other, especially an Other that is hostile, entails sacrifice. It means sometimes experiencing betrayal, rejection, and attacks. The easiest thing is to leave. But Jesus did not do that. He embraced and loved us, the Other, and brought us into a new unity with himself.

Knowing this kind of gracious, sin-covering love gives believers in the gospel of Christ the basis for an identity that does not need superiority and exclusion to form itself. In Christ we have a profound security. We know who we are in him, and that frees us from the natural human impulse to despise anyone who is significantly different from us. This enables us to embrace rather than exclude those who differ from us, and that especially goes for our spouse, with all his or her mysterious and often infuriating differences.

This is one part of the glory of marriage, in the Biblical conception. Two people of different sexes make the commitment and sacrifice that is involved in embracing the Other. It is often painful and always complicated, but it helps us grow and mature in ways no other experience can produce, and it brings about deep unity because of the profound complementarity between the sexes.

The Meaning of Marriage, pp. 206–8

1. Whether you are single or married, explain how the selfless love Jesus gives us empowers you to serve in the role God has called you to right now.

2. What do you think God is calling you to believe and/or do in response to what you've learned in this session?

READ FOR NEXT TIME

Read chapter 7, "Singleness and Marriage," in *The Meaning of Marriage*. Also read the Introduction to the next session, "Singleness: Strengthening the Spiritual Family."

MARRIAGE PLAN

To be completed as a couple between group sessions. Remember, the Marriage Plan is best discussed while away from the normal distractions of your married life, whatever they may be. While we recommend these conversations take place on a date night, the main point is to ensure you have an agreed-upon time you've set aside to engage the Marriage Plan.

DEFINING YOUR ROLES

In chapter 6, "Embracing the Other," in *The Meaning of Marriage*, Kathy Keller said:

> The basic roles—of leader and helper—are binding, but every couple must work out how that will be expressed within their marriage. The very process of making these decisions is a key part of what it is to think out and honor your gender differences.
>
> *The Meaning of Marriage*, p. 211

In this session's Marriage Plan exercise you will be discussing the roles you play as husband and wife in your marriage. Use the following questions to develop a plan for how you will begin to practically live out those roles in everyday life.

1. What did the roles of husband and wife look like in the home I grew up in?

2. Based on what we've read and discussed, what do we believe the Bible says about the roles of husbands and wives?

Husbands:

Wives:

3. In our marriage, what one or two steps can we take to help each other start to live out our roles in our marriage? (For example: What family decision is in front of you? How can the wife foster her husband's leadership in family decisions? How can the husband cultivate an atmosphere that empowers his wife to be a true helper in this decision? How might the current division of labor be shifted to make better use of your respective gifts and help the other fulfill their role?)

SINGLENESS
Strengthening the Spiritual Family

HOME STUDY

Read the Introduction in preparation for the Session 4 Group Time. Also read chapter 7, "Singleness and Marriage," in The Meaning of Marriage *if you haven't already.*

INTRODUCTION

I (Spence) have served as a pastor in two churches in cities in the southeastern U.S. where the single adult population is equal to or greater than the married contingent. In both areas, however, it is still somewhat expected (mainly by the Boomer generation) that once you reach a certain age you *should* be getting married. If you pass that age, people begin their not-so-subtle diagnostics to figure out exactly what your defect is. This narrative, however well-meaning, unwittingly reflects a vision of the single life that is neither compelling nor biblical.

On the other end of the spectrum, many inside and outside the church are following a vision for singleness that sees marriage as an outdated social construct. These marital pessimists equate marriage with bondage and singleness with autonomy. And entire social scenes are built to accommodate and exploit these perceived freedoms.

Competing perspectives on the single life in our day create a fog that makes God's vision for singleness hard to see. Fortunately, Scripture provides a compelling vision for the growing population of singles, including those who stay single for life. We know from our study to date that the Bible has a very high view of marriage. Let's not forget that it also exalts singleness, not as a pathway to freedom for ourselves but as a platform for unimpeded service to the family and work of God. His vision for singleness calms the anxious, inspires the skeptical, and empowers the Christian for a single life that is far more than just a "waiting room" for marriage.

The goal of this session is to explore a biblical vision for singleness that is rooted in and dependent upon the most unique of all relational networks: the church family. The church is a place where all people, regardless of marital status, have the privilege to complement and build up one another to love Jesus, our true spouse, and do his work in the world.

GROUP TIME

REVIEW

Session 3 brought the group to the topic of gender roles. The session attempted to give us the ability to see the glory of God in the distinctly different roles held by husbands and wives in a marriage.

- Do you have any follow-up questions about gender roles?
- How did your conversation around the Marriage Plan go? Did you have any success agreeing on changes to roles?

OPENING QUESTION

What is the most memorable thing anyone has ever said to you about being single? Was it helpful?

VIDEO PRESENTATION

Watch the video for Session 4: "Singleness: Strengthening the Spiritual Family." Use the space provided to take notes on any ideas that stand out to you. Your discussion to follow will review and seek to apply the main ideas of the session.

Notes

DISCUSSION

The following questions are designed to help the group process the ideas from the video, the Bible, and chapter 7 of the book The Meaning of Marriage. *The goal is to begin applying these ideas to your life.*

1. How would you summarize the perspective on singleness presented in the video?

2. Both Katherine and Tina talked about how different their lives were as single people before and after coming to faith. Did anything they said resonate with your own experience as a single adult?

3. If the church is to be a beautiful community including married men and women and single men and women, what are healthy ways men and women in the church can be friends?

4. Churches often unintentionally segregate married and single people in unhelpful ways. What are some practical things your group can do to promote in a non-patronizing way the life-giving interaction of married and single people in your church?

5. In the chapter you read for this session, the authors cited 1 Corinthians 7 (a portion printed below) as a key passage in understanding God's vision for singleness. Describe the perspective Paul is giving to both married and single people in this passage.

> Because of the present crisis, I think that it is good for a man to remain as he is. [27] Are you pledged to a woman? Do not seek to be released. Are you free from such a commitment? Do not look for a wife. [28] But if you do marry, you have not sinned; and if a virgin marries, she has not sinned. But those who marry will face many troubles in this life, and I want to spare you this.
>
> [29] What I mean, brothers and sisters, is that the time is short. From now on those who have wives should live as if they do not; [30] those who mourn, as if they did not; those who are happy, as if they were not; those who buy something, as if it were not theirs to keep; [31] those who use the things of the world, as if not engrossed in them. For this world in its present form is passing away.

[32] I would like you to be free from concern. An unmarried man is concerned about the Lord's affairs—how he can please the Lord. [33] But a married man is concerned about the affairs of this world—how he can please his wife—[34] and his interests are divided. An unmarried woman or virgin is concerned about the Lord's affairs: Her aim is to be devoted to the Lord in both body and spirit. But a married woman is concerned about the affairs of this world—how she can please her husband. [35] I am saying this for your own good, not to restrict you, but that you may live in a right way in undivided devotion to the Lord.

1 Corinthians 7:26–35

> Marriage should not be a strictly individual, unilateral decision. It is too important, and our personal perspective is too easily skewed. The [church] community has many married people in it who have much wisdom for single people to hear. Singles should get community input at every step of the way when seeking marriage.
>
> *The Meaning of Marriage*, p. 248

6. If you are married, whom did you involve in deciding to marry your spouse? To everyone: Why is it important to invite some of your church family into the decision of whether (and whom) to marry?

7. Kathy said in the video conclusion, "Jesus is our true spouse and being single in this life actually puts an emphasis on that which can be missed [if you are married]." What kinds of activities and pursuits is she talking about? How can a local church help empower a single person to this end?

8. The quote Jeff read from Wesley Hill's book* speaks of agonies that come through singleness and marriage but reminds us that we are promised a future resurrection. What are your hopes for this future resurrection? If you were to daydream about our future resurrection, what would you dream about?

CLOSING PRAYER

Close your discussion by praying together as a group, asking with grace and humility for God's help in applying what you've learned in this session.

* *Washed and Waiting* (Zondervan, 2010).

HOME STUDY

PERSONAL REFLECTION

Read the following excerpt from The Meaning of Marriage *and then answer the questions provided.*

This high view of marriage tells us that marriage, therefore, is penultimate. It points us to the Real Marriage that our souls need and the Real Family our hearts were made for. Married couples will do a bad job of conducting their marriage if they don't see this penultimate status. Even the best marriage cannot by itself fill the void in our souls left by God. Without a deeply fulfilling love relationship with Christ now, and hope in a perfect love relationship with him in the future, married Christians will put too much pressure on their marriage to fulfill them, and that will always create pathology in their lives.

But singles, too, must see the penultimate status of marriage. If single Christians don't develop a deeply fulfilling love relationship with Jesus, they will put too much pressure on their *dream* of marriage, and that will create pathology in their lives as well.

However, if singles learn to rest in and rejoice in their marriage to Christ, that means they will be able to handle single life without a devastating sense of being unfulfilled and unformed. And they might as well tackle this spiritual project right away. Why? Because the same idolatry of marriage that is distorting their single lives will eventually distort their married lives if they find a partner. So there's no reason to wait. Demote marriage and family in your heart, put God first, and begin to enjoy the goodness of single life.

The Meaning of Marriage, pp. 226–27

1. If you are single, would you say you are enjoying the goodness of single life the way the Kellers talk about in this excerpt? Why or why not?

2. If you are married, where does your marriage rank in your heart right now? Above or below your relationship with God? How would your daily schedule and prayer life speak to that question?

3. What one or two things do you sense God calling you to apply from this session?

READ FOR NEXT TIME

Read chapter 8, "Sex and Marriage," in *The Meaning of Marriage*. Also read the Introduction to the next session, "Sex: The Act of Covenant Renewal."

MARRIAGE PLAN

To be completed as a couple between group sessions. Remember, in an ideal situation you and your spouse will discuss and work through the marriage plan while out on a date together, away from the normal distractions of everyday life.

FINDING YOUR PLACE IN THE CHURCH FAMILY

Read Hebrews 10:19–25 below:

Therefore, brothers and sisters, since we have confidence to enter the Most Holy Place by the blood of Jesus, [20] by a new and living way opened for us through the curtain, that is, his body, [21] and since we have a great priest over the house of God, [22] let us draw near to God with a sincere heart and with the full assurance that faith brings, having our hearts sprinkled to cleanse us from a guilty conscience and having our bodies washed with pure water. [23] Let us hold unswervingly to the hope we profess, for he who promised is faithful. [24] *And let us consider how we may spur one another on toward love and good deeds,* [25] *not giving up meeting together, as some are in the habit of doing, but encouraging one another — and all the more as you see the Day approaching.*

Hebrews 10:19–25, emphasis added

While this session was on singleness, you probably picked up on the theme of the interdependence of single people, married couples, and families in the spiritual family of the church. God designed the church so that people at each "age and stage" contribute something essential and unique to one another and to the church's mission as a whole.

In this session's Marriage Plan you are going to create an action plan for how you can better relate to a local church family, in particular with people in different marital stages. The goal is not to create a burden for yourselves but to better position your marriage to thrive among the relationships God intended for you. Here are a couple of things to remember as you get started.

- **Take baby steps.** Regardless of whether you've been in the same local church for twenty years or you do not have a church at all, you need to take sustainable baby steps in this part of the Marriage Plan. If you try to do too much, you will likely burn out and slip back to where you are now. Small, sustainable steps over time will be far better for your marriage and your church.
- **Get some outside input.** If you are going to get more involved in your local church, it will help to know what that involvement can look like. So check in with a pastor or someone you know to figure out what the opportunities to participate in community look like.

Here are your questions to discuss as a couple:

1. Who are a few single people in our church we could invite to a meal sometime in the next month as a way to cultivate new friendships?

2. Who in our church is in a life stage we see ourselves entering in the future? How might we connect with them?

3. Who in leadership at our church can we ask to learn more about encouraging interaction between single and married people in our church? (Perhaps you could share a vision with them about the life-giving power of friendships in the local church between people in all stages of life.)

4. Based on the above, what is the next step of involvement in our local church for us as a married couple?*

---

* If you are thinking, "I don't have a church!" don't worry. Talk with other members of this study about their local church and attend with them. It often helps to see a familiar face when you first check out a new church.

SEX
The Act of
Covenant Renewal

HOME STUDY

Read the Introduction in preparation for the Session 5 Group Time. Also read chapter 8, "Sex and Marriage," in The Meaning of Marriage *if you haven't already.*

INTRODUCTION

The first time I (Spence) read the Old Testament book Song of Solomon (or Song of Songs as it's called in some Bible translations) I was eighteen years old. It wasn't that my parents prohibited it or anything like that; I had just never really cared much about the Old Testament. During my freshman year of college I found myself in a Bible study where the leader challenged my general disregard for the first two-thirds of the Bible by telling me to read Song of Solomon. Based on the Bible's table of contents I had always assumed it was something like a Proverbs bonus track. Same author, extra material. Then I read it. At first it was weird because the metaphors were going right over my twenty-first century head. Then I read it again with a commentary that explained what was being said. Whoa! I kept thinking things like, *How did this get in the final edition of the Bible?* and *Does Jesus know this is back here?* I was reading erotic poetry ... in the Bible.

Many people are as surprised as I was to find out how positively the Bible speaks about sex. Maybe because it is an old book or because it is considered a sacred religious text, "may her breasts satisfy you always" is just not something one expects to read in the Bible.

Not only does the Bible talk about sex, it offers a vision for sexual intimacy unlike anything else from its time—or really any other time, for that matter. God designed sex between married partners to be passionate and erotic, intimate and secure, selfless and unifying. God designed it to be so good it gives us an otherworldly glimpse of heaven itself.

Whether you have been long familiar with the Christian sex ethic or this is your first time encountering it, it is especially important in this session that every participant brings an open mind and a generous willingness to understand everyone's viewpoints and personal stories. Notice how this posture is modeled in the video discussion.

GROUP TIME

REVIEW

In the last session, "Singleness: Strengthening the Spiritual Family," the group discussed how a single person can serve and be served by the local church family.

- Did the Group Time and Home Study give you any new insight into how you can think about single people in your local church community?
- If you are single, how did the last session change your view of marriage and your calling as a single person?
- If you are married, how did the last session change the way you interact with your single friends?

OPENING QUESTION

This session's topic is about sex. Did anyone ever have the "sex talk" with you? How did that go? Perhaps it was an awkward parent talk, or maybe it occurred in a sixth-grade health class. How did *you* learn about sex?

VIDEO PRESENTATION

Watch the video for Session 5: "Sex: The Act of Covenant Renewal."
Use the space provided to take notes on any ideas that stand out to you.
Your discussion to follow will review and seek to apply the main ideas
of the session.

Notes

DISCUSSION

The following questions are designed to help the group process the ideas from the video, the Bible, and chapter 8 of the book The Meaning of Marriage. *The goal is to begin applying these ideas to your life.*

1. Did any part of the video discussion connect closely with a part of your story either past or present?

2. In the video, Tara talked about the way present-day culture can warp our expectations for sex. What are some expectations surrounding sex that you brought (or are likely to bring) into marriage that have been influenced by your surrounding culture?

> The modern sexual revolution finds the idea of abstinence from sex till marriage to be so unrealistic as to be ludicrous.... But the Bible does not counsel sexual abstinence before marriage because it has such a low view of sex but because it has such a lofty one. The Biblical view implies that sex outside of marriage is not just morally wrong but also personally harmful. If sex is designed to be part of making a covenant and experiencing that covenant's renewal, then we should think of sex as an emotional "commitment apparatus."
>
> *The Meaning of Marriage*, p. 259

3. In both your reading for this week and in the video, the Kellers presented the idea that reserving sex for marriage reflects a lofty view of sex. This idea runs contrary to the suppressive attitude often attributed to the church when it comes to sex. How could having a "lofty view" of sex affect your own view of sexual abstinence outside marriage?

4. The question many within the church are asking surrounding sexual abstinence seems to be: How can the Christian who is single find a fulfilling life without sex? What are your thoughts?

5. The Bible seems to be clear that within marriage, sex should be a regular and pleasurable part of life. Read 1 Corinthians 7:3–5 and Proverbs 5:18–19 (printed below). How do married couples at times struggle to enjoy the "erotic marriage" the Bible prescribes for them?

> The husband should fulfill his marital duty to his wife, and likewise the wife to her husband. [4] The wife does not have authority over her own body but yields it to her husband. In the same way, the husband does not have authority over his own body but yields it to his wife. [5] Do not deprive each other except perhaps by mutual consent and for a time, so that you may devote yourselves to prayer. Then come together again so that Satan will not tempt you because of your lack of self-control.
>
> 1 Corinthians 7:3–5

> May your fountain be blessed, and may you rejoice in the wife of your youth. [19] A loving doe, a graceful deer—may her breasts satisfy you always, may you ever be intoxicated with her love.
>
> Proverbs 5:18–19

> I believe this particular part of 1 Corinthians 7 is an important practical resource. Each partner in marriage is to be most concerned not with getting sexual pleasure but with *giving* it. In short, the greatest sexual pleasure should be the pleasure of seeing your spouse getting pleasure.
>
> *The Meaning of Marriage*, pp. 267–68

6. Having a selfless, other-first approach to sex can be counter to our impulses. How does the gospel give us both the model and the power for a selfless sex life?

7. What attitudes or expectations do you need to change to begin living out a more other-first approach to sex?

CLOSING PRAYER

Close your discussion by praying together as a group, asking with grace and humility for God's help in applying what you've learned in this session.

HOME STUDY

PERSONAL REFLECTION

Read the following excerpt from The Meaning of Marriage *and then answer the questions provided. You may want to just reflect on the questions mentally without writing down the answers.*

Finally, strike a balance with regard to your sexual thoughts and desires. Some Christians feel deeply stained and defiled by any strong sexual thoughts or daydreams. Others indulge them. The gospel is neither legalism, nor antinomianism. Christians are not saved by obeying God, and yet true salvation will lead to obeying God, out of gratitude. This should lead to a very balanced approach to thoughts and temptations. Martin Luther, for example was reputed to say about sexual desires, "You can't stop birds from flying over your head, but you can stop them from making nests in your hair." By that he meant that we can't stop sexual thoughts from occurring to us — they are natural and unavoidable. However, we are responsible for what we do with those thoughts. We must not entertain and dwell on them.

And if we do something that is sexually wrong, we should use the gospel of grace on our consciences. That gospel will neither take the sin lightly nor lead you to flagellate yourself and wallow in guilt indefinitely. It is important to get the gospel's pardon and cleansing for wrongdoing. Often it is unresolved shame for past offenses that stir up present, obsessive fantasies.

The Meaning of Marriage, pp. 262–63

1. The temptation to sexual gratification outside of marriage attacks both the married and the single person. What kinds of sexual temptation are you facing right now?

2. The first step to freedom from any kind of sin is repentance. That is, acknowledging to God what you've done as sin — and then turning away from it and toward him. He enables you to do this through the forgiveness he offers in the gospel. Repentance is not just feeling sorry but changing the direction of your heart's affections. In true repentance you begin to see Jesus as more desirable than the sin you thought you were finding satisfaction in. Only God's Spirit can provide lasting change, but such change begins as you choose the glory of God over the faux glory of sexual sin.

   For what sexual sin do you need to begin the process of forgiveness and repentance?

3. In a society so immersed in sex, it is quite common for people to have sexual experiences that have left them feeling powerless and wounded — whether from trauma, such as rape, abuse, or betrayal; or more nuanced things, such as disappointment caused by a former sexual partner. One effect of sin is for its victims to feel shame and isolation, but the gospel offers healing in community, and that can often begin with talking to someone about it. It will be a step of courage to choose to talk with someone, but the result can be to move you closer to the freedom you've been hoping for.

For what pain from the past do you need healing? Do you have a trusted confidant you can share your experience and feelings with?

READ FOR NEXT TIME

Read chapter 4, "The Mission of Marriage," in *The Meaning of Marriage*. Also read the Introduction to the next session, "Hope: Seeing the Great Horizon."

MARRIAGE PLAN

To be completed as a couple between group sessions.

A BIBLICAL CHECKUP FOR YOUR SEXUAL INTIMACY

No marriage plan would be complete without getting into the topic of sexual intimacy. As acknowledged in the Group Time and in the reading, sex is a powerful force God has created and prescribed for marriage. Reread 1 Corinthians 7:3–5:

> The husband should fulfill his marital duty to his wife, and likewise the wife to her husband. [4] The wife does not have authority over her own body but yields it to her husband. In the same way, the husband does not have authority over his own body but yields it to his wife. [5] Do not deprive each other except perhaps by mutual consent and for a time, so that you may devote yourselves to prayer. Then come together again so that Satan will not tempt you because of your lack of self-control.   1 Corinthians 7:3–5

There is no way to obey this command of Scripture and maintain a dormant sex life as a married couple. This session's Marriage Plan is designed to help you take a step toward having a regular, active marital sexual partnership. Because every couple is different, a one-size-fits-all approach cannot work here. The goal is to help you take *a* step. It is up to you to build from there.

As in previous sessions, this discussion works best in a setting away from the normal distractions of your everyday life. Use the following questions to help you come to agreement on your next step toward experiencing the regular, active sexual intimacy God wants for your marriage.

1. Do you believe our current sex life fully agrees with Paul's admonition in 1 Corinthians 7:3–5?

2. What is one *internal* factor in our marriage we need to address to move closer to God's vision for our sexual and emotional unity? (For example: unresolved conflict, lack of relational connectedness, physical ailments, etc.) Limit your answer to one thing. Because people are flawed and marriage is dynamic, it would be impossible to wait until you are perfect to have sexual intimacy. But you can work toward a better marriage as you work toward sexual intimacy.

3. What is one *external* factor in our marriage we need to address to move closer to God's vision for our sexual and emotional unity? (For example: children, work hours, Uncle Bob still lives in the guest room, television and Internet distractions, etc.) As with the previous question, limit your answer to one thing.

4. Knowing we will *both* have to have a selfless perspective to achieve greater intimacy, what is one step we could take to move in that direction? (For example: a weekend getaway, scheduled date nights, no TV or Internet after 8 p.m., have sex tonight, move out Uncle Bob, etc.)

5. Having open, clear dialogue is important in developing lasting sexual intimacy. How could we begin to talk more openly and candidly with one another about this area of our marriage?

SESSION 6

HOPE
Seeing the Great Horizon

HOME STUDY

Read the Introduction in preparation for the Session 6 Group Time. Also read chapter 4, "The Mission of Marriage," in The Meaning of Marriage *if you haven't already.*

INTRODUCTION

Pastors sometimes joke with couples that the wedding ceremony is beautiful but deceptive. Beautiful because of how radiant the bride, groom, and all their loved ones look, but deceptive because they will never look so glorious again. We all know that this joke strikes close to home. After all, anyone who has been married for a little while knows the glamour of the wedding day is replaced with the grind of workdays, illnesses, arguments, and takeout after a meal burned on the stovetop. Eventually many married couples drift into accepting their wedding day as a memory immortalized in pictures displayed around the house.

What if instead of your wedding being a memory of your best day, it becomes a preview of how glorious you will be one day in the future? The Christian faith carries the hope of heaven—that one day we will be in the holy, spotless presence of Jesus and will ourselves be holy like him. That perfect, glorious self is something we only see glimpses of here on earth, and your spouse is the most likely person to catch those glimpses. As great as their physical beauty may be, there will be even greater moments when the image of Christ shines clear and bright in their character like the sun's unexpected rays piercing the sky on an otherwise cloudy day.

God gave Courtney (Spence's wife) the spiritual gift of serving others. Sometimes I think it is hardwired into her DNA to see a need and figure out how she can meet it. Often my (Spence's) first reaction is to wonder what that need will cost me personally in time, money, or emotional capital. Of course my cost-benefit analysis can stifle Courtney's serving spirit. In the moments when I step out of the way and she gets down into the grime of a mess with someone, I will sometimes see the sun break through and the image of Jesus is all over her. This is the person God is molding my spouse into, and I am in a better position than anyone else on earth to help her get there!

The purpose of marriage, this session suggests, is to begin to see the person God is making your spouse into, and then to do everything you can to help them toward that future image.

GROUP TIME

REVIEW

The previous session, "Sex: The Act of Covenant Renewal," connected the sexual intimacy between a husband and a wife with the covenant their marriage was founded on. The Bible regards the pleasure found in the marriage bed as far greater than any sexual intimacy to be found outside of it.

- Did anything from your Home Study and/or Marriage Plan help you get a better understanding of the ideas from the last session?
- Are there any ideas you are struggling with from that session, or questions you still want to ask?

OPENING QUESTION

Chapter 4 opens with the question, "What is marriage for?" Before you watch the video, discuss that question. What do you believe marriage is for? What have others told you marriage is for? What is a "successful" marriage?

VIDEO PRESENTATION

*Watch the video for Session 6: "Hope: Seeing the Great Horizon."
Use the space provided to take notes on any ideas that stand out to you.
Your discussion to follow will review and seek to apply the main ideas
of the session.*

Notes

DISCUSSION

The following questions are designed to help the group process the ideas from the video, the Bible, and chapter 4 of the book The Meaning of Marriage. *The goal is to begin applying these ideas to your life.*

1. Many important ideas were brought up in the video. Which one stood out to you and why?

2. Though it is common for people to talk about physical chemistry, in the video Tina named friendship as a type of chemistry as well. What makes friendship so much more powerful of a foundation to build a marriage on than the experience of physical chemistry?

> Within this Christian vision for marriage, here's what it means to fall in love. It is to look at another person and get a glimpse of the person God is creating, and to say, "I see who God is making you, and it excites me! I want to be a part of that."
> *The Meaning of Marriage*, p. 132

3. In the video as well as the book, the phrase "great horizon" was used to describe our view of the future person God is making your spouse into. How could this idea of looking toward your spouse's "great horizon" change the way you look at your spouse today? If you are single but want to be married, how does this change the way you look for a spouse?

4. Read Ephesians 5:25–27 (printed below). The apostle Paul connects the sanctification effect of the gospel (the "chiseling away" to become more like Jesus) to the mission of marriage. This mission, especially for the husband, is to love his wife in such a way that it makes her more beautiful and holy over time. Have you ever seen this kind of love modeled? If so, how?

Husbands, love your wives, just as Christ loved the church and gave himself up for her [26] to make her holy, cleansing her by the washing with water through the word, [27] and to present her to himself as a radiant church, without stain or wrinkle or any other blemish, but holy and blameless.   Ephesians 5:25–27

> Paul … gives his readers a vision for marriage that must have completely astonished them. The primary goal of Christian marriage is not social status and stability, as it was in ancient cultures, nor is it primarily romantic and emotional happiness, as it is in our culture today. Paul points husbands to Jesus' sacrificial love towards us, his "bride." But Paul does not stop there; he goes on to speak of the goal of that sacrificial love for his bride. It is "to sanctify her" to "present her to himself" in radiant beauty and splendor, to bring her to be perfectly "holy and blameless." He wants the new creation for us! He wants to remove all spiritual stains, flaws, sins, and blemishes, to make us "holy," "glorious," and "blameless."
>
> *The Meaning of Marriage*, p. 128

5. The reading for this session introduced the idea of "pseudo-spouses"—things to which you give priority, and maybe even affection, before your spouse. Though they may be good things, they sit in a seat designed only for your spouse and thus are toxic to your marriage. What are the most likely things in your life to slip into that "pseudo-spouse" seat, and why do they present such a threat to your marriage? If you are not married and want to be, what priorities in your life do you expect will have to change to keep them from turning into pseudo-spouses?

> Your marriage will slowly die if your spouse senses that he or she is not the first priority in your life. But only if your spouse is not just your lover and financial partner but your best friend is it possible for your marriage to be your most important and fulfilling relationship.
>
> *The Meaning of Marriage*, p. 138

6. In the video, Tim and Kathy as well as Katherine and John shared how they have changed for the better in the course of their marriages. What are some ways your marriage has changed you for the better? If you are single, what are some ways that very close friends have helped you change for the better?

STUDY REVIEW

As you are about to complete The Meaning of Marriage *study, use the two questions below to take a step back and review what God is teaching you.*

7. As you think about these past six sessions, what big ideas are sticking with you? Why?

8. What one or two action steps do you intend to build into your life as a result of this study?

> What, then, is marriage for? It is for helping each other to become our future glory-selves, the new creations that God will eventually make us.
>
> *The Meaning of Marriage*, p. 131

CLOSING PRAYER

Close your discussion by praying together as a group, asking with grace and humility for God's help in applying what you've learned in this session.

HOME STUDY

This final Home Study is intended to help you reflect on the ideas from Session 6 as well as your overall experience with The Meaning of Marriage.

PERSONAL REFLECTION

Read the following excerpt from The Meaning of Marriage *and then answer the questions provided.*

Nevertheless, at the end of the day, Christ's love is the great foundation for building a marriage that sings. Some who turn to Christ find that his love comes in like a wave that instantly floods the hard ground of their hearts. Others find that his love comes in gently and gradually, like a soft rain or even a mist. But in any case, the heart becomes like ground watered by Christ's love, which enables all the forms of human love to grow.

"Dear friends, let us love one another, for love comes from God.... Whoever does not love does not know God, because God is love.... This is love: not that we loved God, but that he loved us and sent his son as an atoning sacrifice for our sins. Dear friends, since God so loved us, we also ought to love one another. No one has ever seen God; but if we love one another, God lives in us and his love is made complete in us" (1 John 4:7–8, 10–12).

The Meaning of Marriage, p. 276

1. In what ways do you sense God revealing his love afresh to you?

2. The love of God for us becomes the love that flows through us and out to others. Our spouse should be the first to receive that love. In what new ways is God calling you to love and serve your spouse from an outpouring of God's love in your life? Similarly, if you are single, in what new ways is God calling you to better love and serve those around you?

3. Think back to the Study Review questions (numbers 7 – 8) from the Session 6 Group Time. What do you need to do to begin implementing the action steps you identified?

MARRIAGE PLAN

Here is your last Marriage Plan and perhaps the most romantic of them all. As noted in previous sessions, the Marriage Plan is best applied while out on a date, away from the normal distractions of life.

YOU ARE GOD'S MASTERPIECE

Throughout the session and in the book, the idea of the great horizon kept coming up. Now is a chance to begin building a hope-filled, Jesus-centered vision into your marriage. Kathy used the idea of thinking of your spouse as an unfinished piece of stone that still needs chiseling in order to become the final work of art. She made the important observation that chiseling is always constructive, not destructive. In this Marriage Plan you are going to write out a profile for who you see God making your spouse into — a specific description of their great horizon. Answer the following questions about your spouse to help you create that profile. Avoid generalities in your responses; the more personal you are, the more meaning it will have for your spouse.

1. I see the love of Jesus on display in your life when you _____
   (this is where you see the gospel alive and at work in your spouse).

2. God has clearly gifted you in _____ (this is where you see your spouse really flourishing).

3. As believers, we are promised a future glory—freedom from all of our sins and agonies—when we encounter Jesus face to face. What particular kind of unbridled joy, redemption, and freedom do you envision for your spouse?

NOTES FOR
LEADERS

SESSION 1
SERVICE: MARRIAGE
ISN'T ABOUT YOU

General Note. Several of these questions explore aspects of the core problem with every human being, which the Bible calls "sin." Our natural disposition toward self-preservation creates blinders on our eyes and hearts so that we cannot see the impact of our selfishness on others. One effect of believing the gospel is that God begins to remove these blinders, and our hearts soften to the point that we can care more about our spouse than we do ourselves. Until we admit our sinfulness and our need for help, we cannot begin to live the kind of lives God offers us in the gospel. The road to a healthy marriage begins in repentance—acknowledging our sin and our helplessness to escape it.

Question 5. In the video, Tim Keller points out that the power to continuously love your spouse comes from the inexhaustible love of God constantly pouring into you. Without the gospel, the idea of trying to constantly love your spouse seems exhausting. There must be an outside source for that love ... and the gospel (the story of what Jesus has done for you in love) is that source.

Question 7. You can never go wrong using the words of Scripture to explain the gospel message. The words of the apostle Paul in Ephesians 2:1–10 clearly spell out that message, as well as what our lives were like before we believed the gospel and how they should change afterward.

SESSION 2
COVENANT: CREATED
TO MAKE PROMISES

Question 3. You may find helpful Tim Keller's comment that identity in Christianity is received, yet in all other religions identity is achieved. The marriage vows are first made to God, in acknowledgment of his providence and of our submission to his will. Then, a couple makes vows to each other that will model the gospel and be empowered by the Holy Spirit. These vows are entirely built on what Christ has done, not what you must do, to begin a relationship with God.

Question 6. The only path of hope for your marriage is the path of humility. Your spouse sees you in both the high-octane emotional moments and in the monotony of your everyday routine. He or she knows you. So in the moment when they speak truth about your life, you've got a choice. You can keep your blinders on and reject your spouse, or in humility you can receive what they have to say. If you will truly listen, what you hear may sting, but you will likely be closer to dealing with the real you, and there is hope that you can then change for the better.

Question 7. Two reasons. First, because your spouse knows you better than anyone else, words of genuine affirmation from him or her carry more weight than they would with anyone else. Sticks and stones may break your bones, but the words of a spouse carry much more power. When a spouse lovingly affirms the character of the other, it can move mountains in the heart. Second, we were created to receive this kind of love. We find it modeled most extravagantly for us in the gospel. The love of God the Father for you and me as his "bride" causes him to look at us as he does Christ. He looks adoringly on his church and speaks affirming, true words of love and life and hope. The gospel is our true groom speaking affirming love to his bride. The more we find our love there, the better we will give and receive it in marriage.

SESSION 3
ROLES: LOVING THROUGH MUTUAL SUBMISSION

Question 2. In the chapter "Embracing the Other," Kathy Keller discusses the absence of a gender-specific task list in Scripture. Because the Bible is written for all cultures in all times, it does not give rules specific to a particular time and place. So we must be careful not to impose cultural norms onto marriages as biblical mandates. Many have experienced pain and even abuse from people doing this very thing. For many, separating certain cultural behaviors and expectations from biblical mandate will take time and great patience. It will be important in your group to acknowledge this and create the expectation of a safe environment to talk about such experiences if, and only if, they choose to.

Question 4. This is the crux of this session and where the respect between a husband and wife must be evident. Two benefits occur when a married couple pursues these roles as reflections of the gospel: (1) *Honoring the spouse*: When the husband and wife both believe their own role and the other's role is a representation of Jesus to them, they will give their spouse the dignity and honor worthy of such a role. (2) *Vision*: Knowing the role that God has designed your spouse to fulfill means you can support and encourage them as they grow into that role. In a sense, you get to be God's voice to them as you affirm their divine calling in your marriage. This creates a sense of direction and vision that can cultivate a shared purpose for your marriage. "In 1 Corinthians 11:3 Paul says directly what is implied in Philippians 2 — namely, that the relationship of the Father and the Son is a pattern for the relationship of husband to wife" (*The Meaning of Marriage*, p. 198).

SESSION 4
SINGLENESS: STRENGTHENING THE SPIRITUAL FAMILY

Review section, second question. You know your group. If this question is either irrelevant or explosive, you can pass on it. The goal of the review, at this stage in the meeting, is just to get people talking.

Question 1. You may be surprised by the different ways your group members summarize the exact same video they just watched together. Affirm your group members for contributing, and then be ready to offer a summary of your own that includes the equality in value God places on both genders, and the implications for singles and marrieds of participating in the spiritual family that is the church.

Question 4. This is a brainstorming question and the answers will differ from group to group. If your group is all singles or all marrieds, you are going to have to go outside of your group to create interaction with people of the other marital status. If your group already has a mix of people, begin thinking how you can interact on a more "family-like" level with one another. Married people must be intentional to open their lives to single people. Single people must embrace their spiritual family and be ready to flex their lives to participate in family life with their married brothers and sisters.

Question 5. From *The Meaning of Marriage*, pages 221–22: "What are the implications of this? On the one hand, it means that all the social and material concerns of this world still exist. The world goes on and we live in it. We must take thought for tomorrow. Yet our assurance about God's future world transforms our attitudes toward all our earthly activities. We should be glad of success, but not overly glad, and saddened by failure, but not too downcast, because our true joy in the future is guaranteed by God. So we are to enjoy but not be 'engrossed' in things of this world. What does this mean for our attitude toward marriage and family? Paul says it means that both being married and not being married are good conditions to be in. We should be neither over-elated by getting married nor over-disappointed by not being so—because Christ is the only spouse that can truly fulfill us and God's family the only family that will truly embrace and satisfy us."

Question 6. This concept may be a surprise to your group members. Because the connection between the church and singleness is not obvious to most, take your time here. An individual must grasp that they are secure in Christ and that God has given them access to a family with deeper roots, the Bible claims, than their biological family. When they grasp that truth, they can begin to be free from the anxiety of needing marriage and also able to participate in the family life they may not have yet through marriage.

When it comes to marriage, the church is the community that can share the joys and burdens of marriage with a couple. The marriage lived out in a network of loving brothers and sisters can be consistently saturated with the hope of the gospel. This is the kind of greenhouse where lasting marriages can grow and flourish.

SESSION 5
SEX: THE ACT OF
COVENANT RENEWAL

General Note. A conversation on sex can be one of the most awkward small group discussion topics. One of the functions of the video you watch before the discussion is to model the nature of the interaction we hope your group will follow. Even though the group in the video includes both men and women, the discussion ends up being very beneficial for everyone involved. (These were not scripted actors, simply people who put some thought into preparing for the discussion.) One way to defuse the potential discomfort your group may feel is to just state it outright at the beginning of your discussion, right after the video. Try saying something like:

"Hey everyone, I know today's discussion is on sex. In order to work toward the life change we are all seeking in this study, I want to challenge you to be somewhat transparent in our conversation tonight. As the leader I will try to model this. About that transparency: If you are married, be transparent in a way that honors your spouse. If you are single, be transparent in a way that honors others you may bring up in your story."

Question 2. Some in your group may come from the "sex is leisure" or "sex is an appetite" perspective here. These people connect with the overall message of present culture being channeled to them. Others, however, may relate more to a private, negative view of sex created by their parents or maybe a religious system of some kind. The goal at this point is to help them identify expectations without judgment.

Question 4. It is no secret that outside *and inside* the church many adults are not practicing sexual abstinence before marriage. The goal of this question is to help unearth that reality without shaming people in a group setting. You must remember that true life change comes when God reveals his ways as better for a person than the way they are currently living. Do not shy away from truth in this discussion, but remember to always speak truth *in love*. If lasting change is going to happen, this conversation will most likely be nothing more than the spark that ignites a much longer, more intense, and personal dialogue between a couple or maybe between you and an individual in the group.

Question 5. This shouldn't be a long discussion. It's a chance to get the obvious things out on the table — kids, busy life, lack of intentionality. It also may yield some other comments such as those mentioned in the video about physical pain or difficulty in sex. Give people a chance to be transparent, but do not let it turn into griping or blaming. Again, remind the group to "honor the other" in their transparency.

Question 6. This is a chance to connect theology to sex. The gospel is the model for a selfless sex life because Jesus gave himself for us, sacrificing himself so that we might receive the reward of salvation. The gospel is the power for an other-first approach to sex because we are promised such satisfaction in Christ that we do not *need* it in the form of sexual gratification from our spouse.

SESSION 6
HOPE: SEEING THE
GREAT HORIZON

General Note. This session picks up on a set of ideas from chapter 4 in *The Meaning of Marriage*, "The Mission of Marriage." Though it may seem out of order to go back to the middle of the book at this point, the content was intentionally held until the end in order to give the members of your group a vision to work toward as they complete this study. Encourage everyone to finish their last Home Study and Marriage Plan even though the group will not reconvene.

Question 2. This question is geared more toward single people than married people. If your group consists only of married people, consider using an alternative form of this question such as, "What can you do to begin cultivating more of a friendship in your marriage than you have currently?" The point here is to begin applying the idea that friendship is a powerful force for a strong, hope-filled, enjoyable marriage.

Question 4. The concept for this session is a little abstract but extremely important. According to Ephesians, marital love is supposed to actually make you into a different person—not just a nicer person, but a more Christlike person. Such a process, like carving a sculpture from a block of marble, takes time and intentionality. Like any aspect of discipleship, having this modeled for you helps you understand what it can look like in your own life. The goal of this question is to bring out any examples of such love to help the group begin to think about ways they can get started with their own "sculptures."

Question 7. This question is asked in such a way as to capture what is sitting at the front of the minds of your group members. Usually, though not always, their initial reaction to this question is a helpful insight that they've been processing over the course of the study. It's highly unlikely that *everything* was most helpful to *everyone*. Our hope is that one or two ideas are beginning to help individuals and married couples move closer to the true and powerful meaning of marriage.

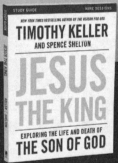
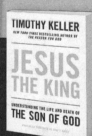

TWO SONS, ONE WHO KEPT THE RULES RELIGIOUSLY
AND ONE WHO BROKE THEM ALL.
ONE FATHER WHO LOVED BOTH LOST SONS BEYOND
ANYTHING THEY COULD IMAGINE.

The Prodigal God curriculum kit contains everything that your church needs to experience a six-week preaching and small group campaign.

In this compelling film and study, pastor and *New York Times* bestselling author Timothy Keller opens your eyes to the powerful message of Jesus' best-known— and least understood—parable: The Parable of the Prodigal Son.

Dr. Keller helps you and your small group or church glean insights from each of the characters in Jesus' parable; the irreligious younger son, the moralistic elder son, and the father who lavishes love on both.

SESSION TITLES:

1. The Parable
2. The People Around Jesus
3. The Two Lost Sons
4. The Elder Brother
5. The True Elder Brother
6. The Feast of the Father

Session one contains the full 38-minute film. Each of the other five sessions will feature a short (2-3 minute) recap segment from the full length film to set up the small group discussion.

THE KIT CONTAINS ONE OF EACH OF THE FOLLOWING:
The Prodigal God DVD, *The Prodigal God* Discussion Guide, *The Prodigal God* hardcover book, and "Getting Started Guide." *Mixed Media Set 978-0-310-32075-3*

ALSO AVAILABLE:
Discussion Guide *(purchase one for each group member) 978-0-310-32536-9*
DVD *(purchase one for each group) 978-0-310-32535-2*
Hardcover book *(available in case lots of 24 only) 978-0-310-32697-7*

PICK UP A COPY AT YOUR FAVORITE BOOKSTORE!

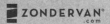

www.redeemercitytocity.com
www.gospelinlife.com

gospel in life is an intensive eight-session course on the gospel and how it is lived out in all of life—first in your heart, then in your community, and then out into the world.

Session 1 opens the course with the theme of the city: your home now, the world that is. Session 8 closes the course with the theme of the eternal city: your heavenly home, the world that is to come. In between, you will look at how the gospel changes your heart (sessions 2 and 3), changes your community (sessions 4 and 5), and changes how you live in the world (sessions 6 and 7).

1 **City** The World That Is

2 **Heart** Three Ways To Live

3 **Idolatry** The Sin Beneath The Sin

4 **Community** The Context For Change

5 **Witness** An Alternate City

6 **Work** Cultivating The Garden

7 **Justice** A People For Others

8 **Eternity** The World That Is To Come

The study guide contains Bible studies, discussion questions on the DVD, and home studies. The home studies consist of a series of readings, quotations, exercises, questions, and projects to help delve deeper into the topic of each session. The guide also includes an extensive section of notes to help leaders prepare.

Gospel in Life Study Guide: 978-0-310-32891-9
Gospel in Life DVD: 978-0-310-39901-8

AVAILABLE ONLINE OR AT YOUR FAVORITE BOOKSTORE!

 ZONDERVAN®
.com

www.redeemercitytocity.com
www.gospelinlife.com

 REDEEMER
CITY to CITY

THE
MEANING
OF
MARRIAGE
Special Offer

Your purchase of this study includes a gift of
two free sermons and a Q&A session on
marriage by Timothy and Kathy Keller.

Visit the address below and use the discount
code to download your free mp3s.

www.GospelinLife.com/MarriageStudyOffer

Discount Code: **KJ8YTP**

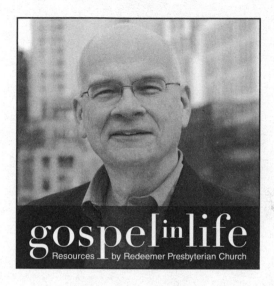

We invite you to visit gospelinlife.com where you can browse 25 years of sermons by Timothy Keller. View the 10 most popular sermon series:

www.GospelinLife.com/Top10

This list includes the most popular Redeemer sermon series of all time, a nine-part series on marriage from Ephesians 5, which was the basis for the best-selling book *The Meaning of Marriage*.